THIS IS ME!

WHISPERS OF IMAGINATION

Edited By Lynsey Evans

First published in Great Britain in 2024 by:

Young Writers
Remus House
Coltsfoot Drive
Peterborough
PE2 9BF
Telephone: 01733 890066
Website: www.youngwriters.co.uk

Book Design by Ashley Janson

Softback ISBN 978-1-83565-063-9

Printed and bound in the UK by BookPrintingUK
Website: www.bookprintinguk.com
YB0574A

FOREWORD

For Young Writers' latest competition This Is Me, we asked primary school pupils to look inside themselves, to think about what makes them unique, and then write a poem about it! They rose to the challenge magnificently and the result is this fantastic collection of poems in a variety of poetic styles.

Here at Young Writers our aim is to encourage creativity in children and to inspire a love of the written word, so it's great to get such an amazing response, with some absolutely fantastic poems. It's important for children to focus on and celebrate themselves and this competition allowed them to write freely and honestly, celebrating what makes them great, expressing their hopes and fears, or simply writing about their favourite things. This Is Me gave them the power of words. The result is a collection of inspirational and moving poems that also showcase their creativity and writing ability.

I'd like to congratulate all the young poets in this anthology, I hope this inspires them to continue with their creative writing.

CONTENTS

THE POEMS

Favourites

If I was a colour, I would be red as a hot fire.
If I was an animal, I'd be a clever penguin.
If I was a season, I would be warm as summer.
If I were a shape, I would be a triangle.
If I were a type of food, it would be a lime-green pear.
If I was a mood, I would be calm.
If I were a subject, I would be history, full of facts.
If I was an object, I'd be playful as a fidget.
If I were a few of my friends, I would be Maisy, Hallie and Zainab.
If I were to pick an exercise, it would be speedy swimming.
If I were a country, I'd be Italy.
If I was a type of hair, I would be thick, silky hair!

This is what I would be and do.

Inaya Khurram Warraich (9)
Anfield Road Primary School, Liverpool

Me

My name is Alice.
I speak another language.
I speak Portuguese and English.
I have a sister.
I love my life.
I have good friends and my BFFs.
I like games and I love dancing and singing.
I love playing with my Kindi Kids.
I love playing with my sister and my BFFs.
I am a little shy and it is a little hard for me to do my work by myself, but I try my best every minute and every second.
My school is the best.
I love learning maths and English and reading stories.
I lived for six years in Brazil.
I love flowers and my favourite colour is light purple.
I have the best BFF in this world, she is called Nadia!
My favourite day in the year is Christmas.
Times tables are hard for me.

I work hard to learn in school.
I love playing on my phone but I really love playing with my family and my Kindi Kids.
I love stories.
This is my story!

Alice Martins (9)
Anfield Road Primary School, Liverpool

I Am Just A Song

A big variety of happiness vinegar, all of its entirety!
You might as well add the whole jar of moody I guess -
Don't forget the red salt, be my guest!
Seven bottles of creativity,
I don't know what's next.
I'm not a good baker but I'm very strong,
You can add that to the recipe,
Five tablespoons won't do you wrong.
All I know is not to leave the cake in the oven too long,
Don't get me wrong, I love a good crisp,
Oh, that reminds me...
I like Spotify... So you might as well call this recipe a *song!*

Sandrine Fumey (10)
Anfield Road Primary School, Liverpool

This Is Me!

Hello, my name is Chloe and I'm from Liverpool
I love all sweets
And love dancing to the beat
I was born in April, yes in spring
I went to school in the flap of a wing
I love the colour sage
Ten is my age
And I can't pick between red roses and white daises
I can't pick between cute poses or dancing all night long
Yes, this is really me and me I shall be
I really love to do things others find new
No one is the same, we all have different ways and aims
So yes, this is me and me I shall always be.

Chloe Holgate (10)
Anfield Road Primary School, Liverpool

Remember Gymnastics

w R ite it down
E ducated mind, don't let it forget
M y work! I can look back
E nthusiastic but calm
M iss, can you help, please
B efore you write it, check it
E lla, can you help, please
R emember to ask the people on your table

G reat
Y ou have fun
M ats
N ever give up
A crobats
S low and steady
T ake your time
I ncredible moves
C razy flips
S turdy on the beam.

Zoe Lee (10)
Anfield Road Primary School, Liverpool

This Is Me

Harry Potter is my jam
Star Wars, though not a fan
Dogs, I have one of my own
Cats make me moan.

Country girl, that is me
I am who I want to be
I love my family and friends
I want to be with them to the end.

I try to mend people's mishaps.

I like school, it's so cool.
Sometimes I wish I rule
Brothers, I like annoying
I always end up winning.

I don't like bling,
It makes my eyes sting.

I am me and who I want to be.
This is me!

Matilda Griffiths (9)
Anfield Road Primary School, Liverpool

My Summer Holidays

My family and I went to Ukraine last summer.
We ate sweetcorn that my grandpa grew for me.
We heard some bats at night.
They were loud. Very loud!
I swam in a pool with my friends.
They were happy and I was happy too!
Last summer was very sunny and hot.
We ate loads of watermelon and many delicious foods.
We went to the forest and saw many plants and beautiful flowers.
Also, we climbed up a hill and saw amazing views of the sunset.
We spent our time together with my family and cousins very well.

Mariam Rusnac (8)
Anfield Road Primary School, Liverpool

Nature Is Everywhere!

I really love nature,
There is nothing that's greater,
From lavender to bluebells,
To living things with shells,
Nature is also air,
Nature is everywhere,
People don't believe it,
They first think and sit,
About problems in life,
Women becoming wives,
But they don't really know,
That nature makes you say *YOLO*,
Nature is the best,
It can help you on a test,
Forget all about stress,
Love nature,
Nature is everywhere!

Rania Cierb (10)
Anfield Road Primary School, Liverpool

What Makes Me

Five teaspoons of giggles
Stir in some science
Warm up some family
Mix in some fun
Put in some rockets
Add in some pink
Freeze some ice cream
Ten millilitres of electronics
Fifty grams of bonfires and fireworks
Add in some nature
Make sure you add in some designing and
organising
A bit of cleaning
Some teaspoons of holidays
Mix in weekends and birthdays
Get some new glasses
Add in some sleeping
And finally, add water parks, waterfalls and green
parks.

Khadijah Zubair (9)
Anfield Road Primary School, Liverpool

Me And My Best Friend David

Me and my best friend,
All around, non-stop playing,
All about one glare turns into a stare.
You should not dare to interrupt our stare.
If you would dare, we will always be there,
Side by side, together,
Our friendship will always be there,
Play with toys all day long,
From tag to football, to basketball,
It goes on forever,
Non-stop playing together,
Together for five whole years,
I will always be there for you,
We will always be there for each other.

Isaac Griffiths (8)
Anfield Road Primary School, Liverpool

This Is Me Rhyme

Hi, my name is Flo
This is my poem, listen to it go.
Sunday morning is for swimming,
In the pool, I like chilling.
I love my mummy,
She buys chocolate for my tummy.
Turtles and koalas, I love them both,
But I can't choose which one I like the most.
My walls are purple and teal,
My turtle teddy, I wish it was real.
Pesto pasta for my tea,
It is very yummy!
I like the beach, I like the sea,
Watching the sunset with a chippy.

Florence Ferry (8)
Anfield Road Primary School, Liverpool

This Is Me

If I were an animal
I'd like to be a rabbit
I'd hop around all day long
Munching on a carrot.

If I were a holiday
I'd be one by the beach
With lots of seashells
For the sea to reach.

If I were a park
I'd be Croxteth Hall
With a farm to visit
Lots of trees standing tall.

But my name is Daisy
I am kind but shy
I like watching films and walking my dog
Green grass and blue skies.

Daisy Ferry (10)
Anfield Road Primary School, Liverpool

A Pinch Of Magic

Hocus pocus, hubble bubble,
Magic always leads to trouble.
Three brave sisters, one fresh start,
How long till it falls apart?

From crown stones, damp and swirling fogs,
To hidden rooms and hopping frogs.
A pretty village, so serene,
But something lurks beneath, unseen.

Shuffle, shuffle, what's that sound?
It's in the air and all around.
A pinch of magic - use it quick!
There's danger here in Pendlewick.

Giscia Sousa (11)
Anfield Road Primary School, Liverpool

I Have One Million Hearts

I love my mom!
I love my hamster!
I love my dad!
I love my brother!
I love my little sister!

And I love my bff!
I have one million hearts and my bff, Alice, is the best.

I love to sing and dance and play with my bff.
It's hard to be me because I have one million hearts.
If you were to be me, you would mess everything up and you would not like the things I like.

Do you like my story?
I hope you do!

Nadia Handerek (9)
Anfield Road Primary School, Liverpool

That's Me!

Hi, I'm Florence
I'm going to tell you all about me!
I'm sweet, kind
I love pandas
I give lots of high-fives
My favourite food is mac and cheese
I'm very strong
I love people as long as they're sweet
I also have a big sister
And a little brother and sister who are both very annoying
But who cares? I love them
Oh, and just so you know, that's me!
Don't forget to tell your friends about me!

Florence Frances Jae Mcpartlin (9)
Anfield Road Primary School, Liverpool

My Life

I am human and this is what I am.
My name is Mason and I am gentle with animals
But get away very quickly, but that's who I am.
I go to the bank on Monday, Tuesday is bath day,
Wednesday I do maths at school,
And Thursday is my favourite day because it's close to Friday.
On Friday I stay up all night watching films.
I am asleep all day on Saturday.
Sunday, Sunday I get back into my bed
I go to school on Monday.

Mason Williamson (9)
Anfield Road Primary School, Liverpool

This Is Me Now!

T errific I try to be,
H ow hard is this to see?
I ntelligent and resilient I am,
S orry, I do not like ham.

I ncredible at learning,
S uperb at exams.

M arvellous at homework.
E xcited by Jude Bellingham.

N evertheless, I make mistakes,
O h, how I adore milkshakes.
W henever I try to eat steaks, I always think of cornflakes.

Chijimnaka Ononye (10)
Anfield Road Primary School, Liverpool

All About Me/This Is Me

Good at listening.
Great at reading.
Likes playing.
Incredible at writing.

T uesdays in school, learn Spanish.
H appy at school.
I am good at playing football.
S ometimes I wish it was winter.

I am good at other sports.
S ometimes I feel like swimming at home.

M aking things in science is fun.
E xercising is what I sometimes do.

Bright Philip (9)
Anfield Road Primary School, Liverpool

Me

I am a girl with brunette hair,
Bright blue eyes, just like the sky.
Lots of friends, they never end,
I love sweets, delicious like treats.

Mind makes destiny,
They are never ever silent.
My age is nine, always kind,
Unique name, sometimes a pain.

Winter is the best,
But I hate tests.
Favourite food is tuna pasta,
When it comes to writing, I am faster.

This is me.

Scarlett Amanda May Clark (9)
Anfield Road Primary School, Liverpool

I Used To Think

I used to think I was ugly but now I think I'm pretty.
I used to think I was dumb but now I think I'm smart.
I used to think everyone lived until 100 but now I don't.
I used to think I didn't need friends but now I do.
I used to think maths was hard and I still do.
I don't need to be perfect and I don't need to know everything.
But one thing we all need is self-confidence.
This is me.

Minna Huang (9)
Anfield Road Primary School, Liverpool

This Is Me

A ll about me
L ove my family
L ove my dog

A nimals are one thing I love
B ut also loved when I learnt how to ride my bike
O ut and about is where I like to be
U p with the birds and down with the sun is how my day runs
T eatime with my family, everyone is filled with glee

M aking art fills my heart
E verything is about me.

Isla Speed (8)
Anfield Road Primary School, Liverpool

Rhyme

The first day of school can be hard for Mum and Dad.
Part of you feels excited, and the other part feels sad.
For many years you've held their hand, and have been their loving guide.
Now you know the time has come to leave them.
But it is only for a little while, as your child will learn and grow.
At the end of every day they will share with you all they know.
So as you walk away, don't worry anymore.

Laksana (9)
Anfield Road Primary School, Liverpool

This Is Me!

You will need:
200ml of moodiness
Cup of love
Dash of sass
100ml of holiday love
Splash of drama
Jug of art
Sprinkle of Halloween fun

How to make me:
Just add a lot of moodiness
Add a cup of love for animals
Add a dash of sass
Add some love for when you go on holiday
Add both of the jugs of love for drama and art
Add a sprinkle of Halloween to top it all off.

Gracie Liu (10)
Anfield Road Primary School, Liverpool

This Is Me

T alented in the sport football.
H appy in everything I do.
I ntelligent and incredible.
S pecial and sweet.

I dentify.
S peedy swimmer.

M agnificent mathematician.
E nergetic and equal.

How to make me:
A sprinkle of happiness,
A spoonful of talent,
Splash of compassion,
And a splash of intelligence.

Eyaad Qamlan (9)
Anfield Road Primary School, Liverpool

Maisie Moo Hoo

Maisie is funny, and Maisie is friendly.
Mummy is the best and so are you.
I am pretty, I am fun and I am friendly.
My birthday is the eleventh of June,
I was born in 2015.
I can do gymnastics and cartwheels.
And my lucky number is eleven
And my favourite word is 'gob'.
On my birthday we can have chocolate, sweets, cake and mostly presents.
And of course, I love my family.

Maisie Lawson (8)
Anfield Road Primary School, Liverpool

End To Start Of My Day

T elevision, what's on Channel 101
H ot cup of tea while watching telly
I ce cream after cup of tea, still watching telly
S chool time, wait, that doesn't rhyme

I ntelligent in maths, I will need that in my SATs
S pelling time, this doesn't have to rhyme right?

M unch time, I mean lunchtime
E nd of the day, hooray!

Ethan Richard-Ubiomo (10)
Anfield Road Primary School, Liverpool

My Dog

My dog's name is Timmy.
I like to play fetch with my dog.
It's a boy.
He stays in our house.
I love my dog.
My dog is good at running.
He runs more than a jet.
I love my dog.
He loves to jump and he has big teeth.
He loves meat and rice.
I've had him for two years.
My dog is brown with black eyes.
I need to make him clean.
I taught him to run.

Ethan Murapa (8)
Anfield Road Primary School, Liverpool

Jayden's Roaring Rhymes

I have a best mate,
To school, I'm never late.
I'm kind of witty,
I don't want a kitty.
I love reading,
I don't like leading.
I am slay,
I say the word, K.
I am loud,
In a crowd.
I like flowers,
My mate is Lexi Bowers.
I am very kind,
I like to eat watermelon rind.
This is me,
I still have no idea how to use my key.

Jayden Phiri (10)
Anfield Road Primary School, Liverpool

This Is Me

Looking back at memories
I hope they never cease
Reading a diary
I remember the past, it said I was kind of mean
But all of that has changed
Loving animals, then art
Sleeping all day in bed
Cooking Italian food until a fire started
Playing games until midnight and swimming in a pool until a kid comes
Going home to see my favourite TV show
This is me.

Jonathan Obazee
Anfield Road Primary School, Liverpool

This Is Me

I am fun,
And I love to run.
I hate rats,
'Cause they are fat.
They are so smelly,
And have big bellies.

I love guinea pigs,
'Cause they are not big.
And I can keep them in a cage,
Where they will not range.

I love bunnies too,
'Cause they hop and are funny.
I am joyful,
And playful.

This is me!

Chikamma Ononye (8)
Anfield Road Primary School, Liverpool

Who I Am

My name is Sajitha.
I love singing, it's my hobby.
I am really good at singing. I feel safe with people I love.
I am Hindu. I love my sister because she is playful, kind, and helpful.
I love my mum because she cooks, supports me and helps me.
I love my dad, he makes me happy when I am sad.
So, my family are the people I love.
So now you know who I am.

Sajitha Sangeedaraj (8)
Anfield Road Primary School, Liverpool

All About Me

I am funny, kind and fun,
If I get work, I'll get it done,
My head is bonkers, silly as well,
I sometimes even travel to hell,
I love my family but not my brother,
We always argue with each other,
I like my eggs runny,
And drizzled with honey,
I dip toast in and wait for my Xbox to begin,
I hate a roast dinner and I'm a great swimmer.

Casper Cahill (8)
Anfield Road Primary School, Liverpool

My Safe Place

Hi, my name is Haseit, my safe place is my family
Because I know they can keep me safe and love me.
They love me and because I know they will always protect me, I feel safe.
My loving family is always there to support me and to help me achieve my dreams
Which obviously shows how kind and supportive they are.
I am so dearly grateful for such an amazing family.

Haseit Birhani Desta (8)
Anfield Road Primary School, Liverpool

Untitled

M oody on Monday
Y ellow on Sunday

N ice on Friday
A t ballet on Saturday
M um makes me exist
E verything is right

I love night
S hine when bright

B orn in July
E ven needs pie
L ove alight
L ike Angel Delight
A nd goodnight.

Bella Clayton (10)
Anfield Road Primary School, Liverpool

My Opinions

D ance is the best
A lyssa is my name
N othing beats the passion of music
C artwheels are fun
E verything is better when I'm dancing

P arties are my favourite too
A party for all
R unning is fun
T alking to my friends is fun
Y ou're gonna find out why very soon.

Alyssa Vine (8)
Anfield Road Primary School, Liverpool

This Is Me

Marshmallows, muffins, milkshakes
Sweets, strawberries, swimming
Sports, singing
Friends and family
When I grow up I want to be a doctor
I'm kind of poor in Roblox but I'm the best diver
I love cleaning my room
I love school
I love summer
I love Christmas
I love dancing
I love YouTube

This is me.

Karen Tinovimba Matseka (9)
Anfield Road Primary School, Liverpool

Things I Like

My name is Anthony
And I climb like a chimpanzee
And I also love to decorate my Christmas tree

I really love Halloween
And my favourite colours are red and green

I really like Bonfire Night
My favourite video game is Fortnite

My favourite sport is football
I'm a morning person and I'm not that tall.

Anthony Ellis (10)
Anfield Road Primary School, Liverpool

This Is Me

I am sporty and kind
I have a super slow mind
Gymnastics is my superpower
And school is my learning shower

I handspring, I round off
I am a lifelong gymnastics fan
I do it wherever I can

I love baking
My back is always aching

I love drama
And my dream holiday is...
To go to the Bahamas.

Emmie Mcgee (10)
Anfield Road Primary School, Liverpool

It's Me

Burgers and cakes.
Swimming and cricket.
Jungles and flowers.
Animals and butterflies, they are super cute.
I love my mum's food and sweets.
I love everyone being nice and I hate mean people.
I love school and games, the colour purple, oh and pink.
I always love having fun.
I love the movies Stitch and Rapunzel.

Yasmine Diona (9)
Anfield Road Primary School, Liverpool

Rhyming

I love my mum
I love football
I love my I96
I love my brother
I love my teacher
I love my sister
I love playing PS7
I love reading
I love jets
I love dogs
I love being king
I love to run
I love Times Tables Rock Stars
I love my friends
I love to race
I love PE
I love swings.

I lyen (8)
Anfield Road Primary School, Liverpool

Ability Lover

A kennings poem

I am a...
Space lover
Halloween dresser
Christmas decorator
Book reader
Super crafter
Ultimate gamer
Helpful leader
Kind counsellor
Artistic painter
Choice maker
Drawing creator
Learning swimmer
I may be quiet and timid...
But you shouldn't assume because my ability has no limit!

Sophie Elizabeth Langan (10)
Anfield Road Primary School, Liverpool

This Is Me!

L exi is my name
O pen to ideas
V ery open-hearted, kind and sweet
E very day I'm happy

F amilies are so sweet
A nd I love to cook
M cDonald's is yummy
I love to look at the yellow ducks
L ove fluffy cats
Y ou are the best.

Lexi-Mae Phythian (10)
Anfield Road Primary School, Liverpool

Recipe To Make Me

To make me, you need:
Fifty spoonfuls of sports
Twenty spoonfuls of games
Five spoonfuls of humour
10 spoonfuls of work
Ten spoonfuls of anime
Ten spoonfuls of snacks
Five spoonfuls of adventure
It's fun if I can remember
Running, running up and down
Like a king about to be crowned.

Ehimen Omovbude (9)
Anfield Road Primary School, Liverpool

My Life

I'm so fun,
I'm so fast,
I hate bugs so I will never touch them,
I love football and animals too,
I'm so angry when I'm hungry.

I like everything, animals and football,
I love snakes and games as well,
I hate bugs and will never touch them,
When I'm happy I play a lot.

Loay Ammar (8)
Anfield Road Primary School, Liverpool

This Is Me

T all for my age,
H air's always a mess,
I ntelligent and friendly,
S ometimes, I struggle but get over it.

I love reading and playing with my dog,
S weet tooth.

M alls and shops are my favourite,
E xamples are great for struggles.

Sienna Palin (10)
Anfield Road Primary School, Liverpool

Sad

When I see the ice cream truck
And I ask my dad, and he says,
"No," and I become sad.

When people don't play with me
And I'm sitting alone, I become lonely.

When they make something
To make me sad.

When my dad doesn't allow me
To play in the park.

Bethel Otaru (8)
Anfield Road Primary School, Liverpool

All About Me

I'm super sarcastic,
My body like elastic,
I'm very artistic,
Sometimes I go ballistic,
I dance and turn,
School is where I learn,
Sometimes I am concerned,
I would love to go to Hawaii,
But the chance is very tiny,
When I am older, I want to perform,
Dancing is my dream.

Amelia Scurrah (11)
Anfield Road Primary School, Liverpool

This Is Me

If I was a colour, I would be green like Mother Nature
If I was a season, I would be summer
If I was a food, I would be a pizza
If I was an animal, I would be a penguin
If I was a sound, I would be rain
If I was an instrument, I would be a guitar
If I was a subject, I would be maths with factors.

Mason Barnes (9)
Anfield Road Primary School, Liverpool

Me

My name's Abdullah
And I run like a cheetah
Every single week
I eat lots of pizza
I'm a good sleeper
When I have a speaker
I'm very loyal
But also a bit spoiled
I play with my mates
And go to lots of states
Enjoying while it lasts
Cos soon it will be past.

Abdullah Nadeem (10)
Anfield Road Primary School, Liverpool

Me

A kennings poem

I am a...
Maths lover,
English writer,
Sports player,
Chocolate eater,
Party planner,
Cake baker,
Cooking lover,
TV watcher,
Clothes designer,
Tea maker,
Good helper,
Decoration maker,
Toy player,
Spring lover,
And finally...
Teacher lover.

Laiba Zameer (10)
Anfield Road Primary School, Liverpool

All About Me

A kennings poem

I am a...
Book reader
School lover
English learner
Maths dreamer
Science creator
Family lover
Art maker
Islam prayer
Friend player
Room decorator
Hijab wearer
Food maker
Swimming learner
Home cleaner
Jet setter
And finally... a good helper.

Somaia Abdalla (10)
Anfield Road Primary School, Liverpool

I Am A Good...

A kennings poem

I am a:
Good drawer
Good listener
Good hand writer
Good talker
Good summer wisher
Good book reader
Good early riser
Good writer
Good chocolate eater
Good tennis watcher
Good wasp fleer
Good jam maker
Good sleeper
Good helper
And finally...

Tori Fisher (11)
Anfield Road Primary School, Liverpool

Signing Is The Best Club

S igning is the best
I t feels like a mystery
G ive me a hint
N othing stops signing
I s this a miracle for life?
N othing will stop me from signing
G iving up is a feeling, not a choice for anyone,
that's why I'm here to help.

Hope Doherty (8)
Anfield Road Primary School, Liverpool

What Makes Me

Playing with my dog
Having fun with my brother
Time on my Xbox
Fortnite of course
Being with my family
I like ice cream with chocolate sauce
Playing football outside
Salt and vinegar crisps
Building Lego models
Watching Sonic the film
This all makes me.

Charlie Garner (9)
Anfield Road Primary School, Liverpool

This Is Me

T rue and kind.
H elpful and nice.
I mage of my mum.
S afe and sound.

I 'm very kind. I'll help you when you are down.
S wimming is my passion.

M oody on Mondays,
E xcept when with my friends.

Darcy Holland (10)
Anfield Road Primary School, Liverpool

This Is Me

Hi, my name is Henry.
My hobbies are football, basketball, games,
Reading, helping people and writing stories.
My favourite things are visiting the salad bar
And spending time in school.
My favourite subjects are maths and computing
(learning challenges).
This is me.

Henry Stinchcomb (8)
Anfield Road Primary School, Liverpool

Make Me!

First, five teaspoons of tea
Next, a cup of sports
A bunch of friends and family
Four spoons of laziness
Two pinches of reading
A bunch of food
Last of all, three spoons of kindness
Blow it a kiss and put it in the oven and bake
There you go, you have me!

Dana Al Motlak (9)
Anfield Road Primary School, Liverpool

Olivia

O livia is my name.
L ove my dog.
I love going to majorettes.
V ery good at dance, gymnastics and swimming.
I n my family, there is my mum, dad, two sisters
and my three brothers.
A nd my nan, grandad, seven cousins and two
aunties.

Olivia Silvey Cantos
Anfield Road Primary School, Liverpool

All About Me

I love red pandas,
I hate rude people,
I love watermelon,
I hate broccoli,
I love chocolate,
I really hate bullies,
I really love my family,
I hate avocados,
I love pizza,
I hate people who think they are better than others,
I love my friends.

Treasure Ugwuewo (9)
Anfield Road Primary School, Liverpool

How To Make Me

Fifty percent of video games and PlayStation
Twenty percent of the time with my dog
Ten percent with my brothers
Ten percent with my family
Ten percent with friends
I am a hundred percent of energy, smiles and a lifetime of football.
And there you have me,

Ianis L Lipan (10)
Anfield Road Primary School, Liverpool

This Is Me!

L ove food, pizza, sandwiches and chips
A rchie is my little brother
C oke and cold drinks
I ce cream, especially on a hot day
E verything, teddies and more.

M usic
A pples
E lephants and Easter.

Lacie Bowers (10)
Anfield Road Primary School, Liverpool

The Foodie In Me

I love to eat pizza with soda for breakfast.
I love to eat chips with ketchup for lunch.
I love to eat popcorn with coconut milk for snack time.
I love to eat crisps with soda for dinner.
I love to eat chocolate waffles and hot chocolate for dessert.

Elsie Richard-Ubiomo (7)
Anfield Road Primary School, Liverpool

My Cats

I have two cats and one is called Emba
He is so cute and he is soft.
The other one is called Lokie, and he is soft as well
And he sleeps between my legs.
Also, he annoys Emba, and then he hisses at Lokie,
But they are so cute sleeping together.

Skyla Abdallah (8)
Anfield Road Primary School, Liverpool

This Is Me

The planet, so icy
The world, so spicy
The smoke, the clouds in the sky
The day, so spicy
The night, so frosty
I don't know why
It's the people so greedy
The place so needy
It's good but
I don't know why.

Ezra Emmanuel (8)
Anfield Road Primary School, Liverpool

I Love

I like football,
I like running,
I love videos that are funny,
I am joyful, playful and hop like a bunny,
I love honey when it is runny,
When I eat it, it fills my tummy,
So do gummies,
And I love learning about Egyptian mummies.

Asanti Hunde (8)
Anfield Road Primary School, Liverpool

This Is Me!

S mile and sing
T uesday is my dancing club
A mazing me and I love my family
C hristmas is coming soon, my favourite day to celebrate
E ating all the food I love
Y ou are stunning the way you are.

Stacey Leon-Ajiboso (9)
Anfield Road Primary School, Liverpool

This Is Me

A ngry and happy
N aff and playful
I love football
M y mum makes me happy
A m so glad because I play out with my friends
L ove school
S ometimes I am sad on Wednesday after school.

Lydia Ball (8)
Anfield Road Primary School, Liverpool

Who Am I

I'm a...
Footballer,
Swimmer,
Basketball player,
Tennis player,
Gamer,
Relaxer,
Traveller,
Sporty person,
Speedy person,
Calm person,
Intelligent,
Kind,
And finally,
Left-handed.

Finley Furness (10)
Anfield Road Primary School, Liverpool

Me!

S miley and happy.
K ind, brave and caring.
Y ou are pretty the way you are, you don't need to change yourself or the way you look.
E ating and drinking the food and drinks I love.

This is me!

Skye Johnston (9)
Anfield Road Primary School, Liverpool

All About Me

In the light, there's a fright,
Snakes I like, in the night.
Every night, I play Roblox,
I have lots of robots.
I hate dogs, a lot,
I love robot dogs, a lot.
I love my friends, a lot,
I hate Brody, a lot.

Eddie Towes (8)
Anfield Road Primary School, Liverpool

Myself

Z hafran is my name
H ave fun at school
A mazing family I have
F ootball is my favourite sport
R oblox is my favourite game
A wesome school I go to
N ever do bad things.

Zhafran Asyraf Firdaus (8)
Anfield Road Primary School, Liverpool

Sadness

My stomach feels empty when I feel this emotion
I start to bite my nails when I feel this emotion
I start to cry when I feel this emotion
I start to take a few deep breaths
What am I?

Answer: Sadness.

Caleb Rossiter (8)
Anfield Road Primary School, Liverpool

The Right Way To Good

R oblox is my favourite game
I am a friendly boy
G aming is my hobby
H ate bullies
T o win.

W inner winner winner
A good life
Y ou'd like me.

Kevin Gibney (8)
Anfield Road Primary School, Liverpool

Recipe!

A dash of kindness
A sprinkle of confidence
A stir of friendship
Bake in some happiness
Add a cup of laughter
Next, add some intelligence
Pour in sprinkles of honesty
Bake in the oven until you have me!

Jessica Smith (9)
Anfield Road Primary School, Liverpool

A Recipe For Me

A dash of love
Add some cuddles
Pour in some fun
Next, add some friendship
Sprinkle in some creativity
A spoonful of beauty
Mix in some energy!
Bake with some oven maker!

And you have me!

Hallie May Bayondie (10)
Anfield Road Primary School, Liverpool

Funny Voice

I sing my song in a funny voice
We all laugh about it
I dance funnily, you laugh about it
I make funny noises
You laugh
I like doing it because it is me
I dance around with people
What emotion am I?

Chikamso Ononye (8)
Anfield Road Primary School, Liverpool

This Is Me

I love pets, cats and puppies,
I love being kind and nice,
I love Miss Riley,
And I love me,
I love learning, I might get a job,
A teacher loves to teach,
A janitor loves to clean,
But I love me.

Comfort Kalu (9)
Anfield Road Primary School, Liverpool

Where It Lies In Your Heart

Where friendship lies
Where it hides in the dark
When someone is lonely
Be friendly
Friendship is the best!
Don't be scared
We are all friends
Make new friends
Friendship is the best!

Noah Griffiths (8)
Anfield Road Primary School, Liverpool

Recipe

A sprinkle of kindness and add some sweetness.
Bake with honesty and incredibleness.
A mixture of happiness, and a cup of helpfulness.
Stir in a lot of friendliness.
Bake me in the oven until you make me.

Mansa Tahir (9)
Anfield Road Primary School, Liverpool

Paulie

P laying with my toys today
A lthough I may not stay
U nique in every way
L ike my family all the way
I n your head you might say
E veryone will want to play.

Paulie Towes (9)
Anfield Road Primary School, Liverpool

A Recipe Of Me

A dash of sadness
Two drops of cheekiness
A stir of humour
And six drops of cleverness
A lot of kindness
And nineteen stirs of lovingness
A little bit of talent
And a lot of calmness.

Muhammad Farhat (10)
Anfield Road Primary School, Liverpool

One Who Identifies Himself Will Identify Almighty

Add some talents
Stir the intelligence
Pour in a bowl of energy
Mix in some maths
Sprinkle in some incredible
Bubble in some helpfulness
Splash a big chunk of kindness
To make me.

Syed Raza (10)
Anfield Road Primary School, Liverpool

I'm A Hero

I'm a hero at maths,
I'm a hero at English,
I'm a hero at being kind,
I'm a hero at football,
I'm a hero, but I'm still learning,
And some people are better than me.

Loay Ammar (8)
Anfield Road Primary School, Liverpool

All About Me!

A sprinkle of love and mischief.
A dash of excitement.
A drop of kindness and sweetness.
Mix it and stir.
Put me in an oven and set it to ten minutes.
A slice of joy and happiness.

Isla Moore (7)
Anfield Road Primary School, Liverpool

I Am

A kennings poem

A football player
A food eater
A sports lover
A game tester
An animal protector
A summer maker
A family favour
A fast learner
And finally
A lazy sleeper.

Shay O'Brien (10)
Anfield Road Primary School, Liverpool

This Is Me

A nimals are the best
N ice and sane
I love school
M ums are the best
A nd play with my dog
L ove my family
S nakes are ugly.

Gloria Szelest (8)
Anfield Road Primary School, Liverpool

This Is Me

If I was an animal, I would be a playful penguin
If I was food, I'd be a warm pizza
If I was a colour, I would be as bright as the sun
If I was an object, I would be a WWE figure.

Elliot Hodgson (10)
Anfield Road Primary School, Liverpool

My Favourite Emotion

My tongue is out my mouth
I'm hopping around like a rabbit
When I'm feeling this emotion
I feel like a baby
My brain switches on the emotion
It feels 100% powerful.

Ruby Martin (9)
Anfield Road Primary School, Liverpool

Eva And Friends

Friends and friends now playing
And having fun in the sun
One day playing
Each in the best
Matching pyjamas
Building snowmen
Being friends
Making friends.

Eva Peloe (8)
Anfield Road Primary School, Liverpool

Kitten

I love my kitten
I like to play with them
I like to bump them with cuddles
I love my mum, my mum loves me
I love to play with my mum
I am lucky that I have them.

Ava Rose Caples (8)
Anfield Road Primary School, Liverpool

Recipe

Add friendship,
Mix in intelligence, with kindness,
Be polite to everybody,
Always listen to whoever is talking,
Be a good problem solver,
Be an animal lover.

Dylan-Graham Morris (9)
Anfield Road Primary School, Liverpool

What Makes You

A kind person I am
Y ellow flowers I love
L ots of friends I have
L ots of love I give to you
A nd my favourite colour is blue.

Aylla Webler (9)
Anfield Road Primary School, Liverpool

My Favourite Thing

My favourite thing is learning
My favourite toy is a toy car
My favourite fruit is an orange
My favourite food is chocolate
My favourite animal is a cheetah.

Nithursan Sivakumar (7)
Anfield Road Primary School, Liverpool

Myself

I love it when I go swimming with my friends.
My favourite animal is a panda.
My favourite colours are purple and blue.
I love to do cartwheels and dance club.

Santiago Castro (9)
Anfield Road Primary School, Liverpool

Recipe To Make Me

What you need:
A dash of love
A sprinkle of talent
Pour in some intelligence
Bake for nine years
You have me!
I will always love this school.

Umer Nadeen (9)
Anfield Road Primary School, Liverpool

Untitled

I am the young one in the family.
I love my family.
I love my friends.
I love Disney.
I love being generous.
And... I love myself... which is me!

Najiwa Ibrahim
Anfield Road Primary School, Liverpool

Sport

S o, be good to win.
P lay your favourite.
O nce you play it, you will love it.
R un in football.
T o be taught sports.

Joseph Holland (8)
Anfield Road Primary School, Liverpool

Accept

I'm a...

Fast runner
I like nature
Fast swimmer
Big adventure
I'm smart
I like Greek mythology

This is me!

Daniel McGrath (10)
Anfield Road Primary School, Liverpool

All About Me

I love making cakes with my mom.
I love my family and teacher.
I love cooking with my mom and friends.
I love playing with my mom and friends.

Mia Martes (7)
Anfield Road Primary School, Liverpool

This Is Me

P retty funny
R esilient
I ntelligent
Y ellow is my second favourite colour
A nd I love my family.

Priya Nelson (11)
Anfield Road Primary School, Liverpool

This Is Me!

D elightful,
E nergetic,
S uper,
T errific,
I ntelligent,
N osy,
Y eehaw!

Destiny-Tiammie Bikarova Bayero (9)
Anfield Road Primary School, Liverpool

Football

I can hear the people shouting my team's name
I can see the football in the goal
I can hear a whistle, that means it's a goal!

Mohammed Ammar (8)
Anfield Road Primary School, Liverpool

All About Me

A kennings poem

I am a...
Family lover
Bracelet maker
Summer dreamer
Cake eater
Art maker
And finally...
A pet keeper.

Willow Evans (10)

Anfield Road Primary School, Liverpool

My Mommy

My mum likes to
Play with me every day
And my little brother
My mommy
Is the best mommy
Ever in the world.

Ariella Gora (9)
Anfield Road Primary School, Liverpool

Who I Am

Sleeping, eating, walking, talking.
Happiness is my favourite thing.
iPad, penguins, pizza, burgers,
La, la, la.

Thomas Price (7)
Anfield Road Primary School, Liverpool

This Is Me

A kennings poem

Big boy
Dog lover
Hard hitter
Good gamer
Amazing swimmer
Power Ranger lover

I am Alfie.

Alfie Robinson (9)
Anfield Road Primary School, Liverpool

I'm Clever

C lever
L istening
E nergy
V ery good
E nergy
R eally good.

Anastasija (8)

Anfield Road Primary School, Liverpool

This Is Me

A kennings poem

Slow swimmer,
Fast runner,
Football player,
Roller skater,
Problem solver,
Friend maker.

Thomas Parkinson
Anfield Road Primary School, Liverpool

Untitled

C ricket is fun
A ctive
I nvested in physics
N ot really invested in cats.

Cain Reynolds (9)
Anfield Road Primary School, Liverpool

What I Love

A kennings poem

Big hugger
Dog lover
Hard hitter
Amazing swimmer
Power Ranger lover
I am Alfie.

Alfie Robinson (9)
Anfield Road Primary School, Liverpool

About Myself

I love gymnastics.
I love my mum.
I love my dad.
I love food.

Bella Seels (8)
Anfield Road Primary School, Liverpool

All About Me

E ager to learn new things.
V ery kind to those around me.
I ndependent in every subject.
E very day, I try my best.

L oyal to my family and friends.
O nly have important reasons to be mad.
R eally brave, each day and every day.
I 'm the best version of me.
M azin' at all of my hobbies.
E xplaining things is my middle name.
R eally positive when people need it.

B eautiful in every way.
U nbelievable handwriting in every book.
X - well, let's not talk about that.
T elling myself I'm the best.
O nly kind people around me.
N o one will ever be me.

Evie Lorimer-Buxton (9)
Hazelmere Junior School, Colchester

The Helpful Gamer

Coming out during the day
Helping people in the dark
And giving the people the light
The gratitude fills the heart of the giver
Despite the harsh life of the person
They always get hated by others
But the gratitude the giver gets allows him to push through the hate from the evil
The brightest light hears about the darkness and brings their dreams to reality
The hated couldn't believe it and became the brightest they could ever be
But they never stopped giving the light they own to the dark who have nothing
The gratitude gets higher and higher and the hater regrets what they did
But their past can't change the person they are now
They have been giving the light already, but they still want more
But all their light is drained away from their past.

Moral: Don't hate others for fun.
Glossary: Light is money and dark is poor.

Temitayo Tijani (9)
Hazelmere Junior School, Colchester

My Best Self

L ife is the best.
A mazing every day.
C omes home happy every day.
E very day is the best.
Y ears of fun memories every day.

T o be happy every day.
Yo **U** are the best.
R ight here for me.
N ow friends forever.
E ver greatest people.
R ewrite the stars every day and night because no one can stop us.

Lacey Turner (9)
Hazelmere Junior School, Colchester

An Acrostic Poem All About Me

I like to dance every day.
S o super at lots.
L ike everyone is different in every way.
A lso, I have the best imagination of the lot.

R eally good at being kind.
O rganising and having lots of fun are things I'm good at.
S o I am always on time when being timed.
E very animal I like, except a cat.

Isla-Rose Cornell (9)
Hazelmere Junior School, Colchester

Difference

D ream job is a doctor
I am special
F un is in my blood
F riends are special
E verything's love
R ight now all I need is God, who's above
E nergetic times
N ow I want to bring all of the great times
C alming music is the best
E xciting times makes me the best of myself.

Joy Mukada (9)
Hazelmere Junior School, Colchester

Myself

L oving in every way
O pportunity standing right in front of me
G rateful every day
A new day, new me
N ever giving up work, no matter what.

B rilliant in a new day
I ncredible in every way
R ight every time
C aring to everyone
H appy, no matter what.

Logan Birch (10)
Hazelmere Junior School, Colchester

About Me

M y favourite colour is purple
I have nice blonde hair
M y favourite game is Roblox because there are loads of games
I am kind and playful

R eally like playing Roblox
O ut of the house finding cool leaves
S uper good at cooking
E asily reading my books.

Mimi Gooch (9)
Hazelmere Junior School, Colchester

Ella Bella Boo

E lla is my name, yeah take that for a ride
L iving like a queen, yeah
L ike I'll never die
A nd no one can take me down, just like that!

M ade for a reason
A nd I'm ruling my own region
I can't change yours, but I've got my opinions.

Ella-Mai Wallace (10)
Hazelmere Junior School, Colchester

Calming Night On Christmas

A s I'm in my room, I spend some time watching my elf.
L aughing with my family while playing.
F inding my cat to try and calm myself.
I 've found my cat, but it's time for dining.
E ven though I'm in my room, I'm still watching my elf on my shelf.

Alfie Easteal (10)
Hazelmere Junior School, Colchester

Me Nathan

N ever sad or feel bad
A nd relax just like his BFF Max
T hough he is sometimes a bit mad
H e is happy just like his sister Cax
A nd he is sometimes mean
N ow time's up, time for me to go, I really enjoy your time.

Nathan Okorodudu (10)
Hazelmere Junior School, Colchester

My Life

Nigeria is where I was born,
On a hot sunny morn.
I live with my nice mom, dad, brothers and sister,
They give my head blisters.
We moved to England last year,
Which I did fear.
But I ended up in Essex,
And glad it wasn't Wessex.

Richard Akindele (9)
Hazelmere Junior School, Colchester

My Skills

D etermined to do my best at all times.
A ltering with the creative wall.
N ativity, creativity, paper plane maker.
I nteresting swimming skills.
E lectric speed to help others.
L ining up to help others.

Ireoluwa Oguntuase (9)
Hazelmere Junior School, Colchester

Amazing Soul

G ood as gold
A mazing every day
B righter than the sun
R ight like my heart
I am in my own world
E very day I make a smile
L ife is like a roller coaster.

Gabriel Omorodion (10)
Hazelmere Junior School, Colchester

My Life

I am nine
I am cool
I am responsible
I am kind
I am myself
I am Louis
Nobody can be like me
No one, no one, nobody in the world can be like me.

Louis Lythgo (9)
Hazelmere Junior School, Colchester

Isla

I 've got mesmerising blue eyes.
S mile that lights up my face
L oves TV
A rt is one of my hobbies.

Isla Rae Moore (9)
Hazelmere Junior School, Colchester

All About Me

A lways energetic
D etermined to succeed
A person that is not pathetic
M y favourite hobby is to read.

Adam Mohamed (9)
Hazelmere Junior School, Colchester

My Lovely Self

R ainbow emotions
U nderstands people when they are sad
B right person
Y es, I can do anything.

Ruby Cooke (9)
Hazelmere Junior School, Colchester

Colourful Emotions

Saffron-yellow buttercups and meadows make me feel happy and joyful
A glowing light inside me makes me skip and leap around
However, once I've reached this glowing height, sadness strikes
No fun in sight
The day takes longer
It's gloomy and I am blue
I feel green, a mixture
When I see something I can't have, I am a green swirl of envy
I am green
A roller coaster of colours rejoins me
And my face can't keep straight
Because when I am excited, a smile has to escape
I am colourful
When I am angry, my face goes hot
Overwhelmed, I can't take the lot
I am red.

Edith Hale (9)
Holy Trinity CE Primary School, Cheltenham

My Home And Heaven Forever

Sometimes I'll sneak out at
Night and lie down under the
Sparkling stars before drifting off
To sleep and then waking with
A start in my beloved jungle
Hammock. Oh, how wonderful it is
To know that it is only Mother
Nature who shares this beautiful,
magical place with me. It is she
Who is the true parent of
The green and blue lizards
That amble about above my
Head, the fiery orange baboons
That shriek at dusk and
Dawn, the vipers that lurk
In the bushes ready to strike
And me. I hear the sound of
All these magnificent creatures
And I begin to feel simply

So wild I became one of
Mother nature's children.
Yet the wilderness is still my home and heaven forever.

Anais Harbinson (8)
Holy Trinity CE Primary School, Cheltenham

But This Is Me

I'm sporty
I like football
I like swimming in the clear blue pool
I like climbing in the sun because it is cool
I like cricket
But this is me.
I am angry
I can be mean
I can get mad
But I have a teddy to squeeze
Like a giant marshmallow
And stress comes out
But this is me.
I am happy
I can be as happy as a puppy with its toy
I have a grumpy grin
And a happy grin
But this is me.
I am sad like a long-lost kitten
I have tears like water
But this is me.

I can be bored
I can be happy
I can be sad
I can be sporty
I can be angry
I can be a rainbow of emotions
But this is me!

Edie Walker (8)
Holy Trinity CE Primary School, Cheltenham

This Is Me

T o start I am happy, I am brave, I am strong and playful.
H ello this is me.
I like school trips when they're good places.
S chool is a wonderful place to learn, especially with a nice teacher.

I like having special moments with family.
S ometimes I am creative, cross, and friendly all at the same time.

M um, Dad, sister and brother, are all special in every way.
E ven though sometimes I shout, I can be nice every day.

Sasha Sandeman (9)
Holy Trinity CE Primary School, Cheltenham

I Am Me

I like going on holiday
Because I almost get to go
To the arcade every day
And I get to see my cousins
And my grandma and grandpa
I love seeing my cousins
I am me
I am almost always happy
And I am sometimes
Really, really sad
I am me
I like doing lots and lots
Of homework
I am me
I really, really love going to the park
I am me
I love surprises
And when it's my birthday
I open my presents
Super-duper fast
I am me.

Jacob Lowicki (8)
Holy Trinity CE Primary School, Cheltenham

My Flowers

T he beautiful flowers are sitting in the garden.
H aving a lovely time in the garden.
I n my living room, I have a bunch of flowers;
they are good.
S taying nice, healthy, and fresh.

I t is a lovely day in the garden.
S ave more money to get new flowers.

M y favourite thing is flowers.
E very single flower is my favourite.

Esperance Attipoe (8)
Holy Trinity CE Primary School, Cheltenham

This Is Me!

T his is me, I love my golden hair
H onestly, I do have a little temper
I llness is what is so against me
S adness makes me quiet, unlike anything else

I love my friends and family
S ee and hope that my friends and family are well

M y concentration on learning is beyond
E xcellent is what I am.

Scarlett Randall (8)
Holy Trinity CE Primary School, Cheltenham

This Is Me

T rees are life
H ate is jealousy
I ce is cold like some people's souls
S tares make me brave

I like being short because I am unique
S miles make me happy and make my day

M e, I am me, I love my family and the smiles they give me
E ating makes me strong and more brave.

Charlotte Rees-Cox (8)
Holy Trinity CE Primary School, Cheltenham

Kendra

K ind, I am kind to other people and my loving family.
E ngaged, I feel engaged for sports day.
N umb, I feel numb when cold and alone.
D reamy, I feel dreamy when asleep.
R andom, I feel random when embarrassed.
A ngry, I feel angry when offended and lash out like a tiger with its prey.

Kendra Bennett-Okunniwa (8)
Holy Trinity CE Primary School, Cheltenham

This Is Me

T his is me, I'm loved by my family
H elp me, I will help you
I am kind, loving, caring, angry, I am a rainbow of emotions
S ometimes I shout when I am angry

I help my family
S ometimes I am sad

M y family love me the way I am
E njoy life.

Amelie Godwin (8)
Holy Trinity CE Primary School, Cheltenham

This Is Me

I am as happy as my dog when we get his lead and go for walks.
I am loved by my family and friends.
I am sad when I lose a toy.
I am angry when my little brother hurts me and sometimes I get him back.
I am four years older.
I am excited when my family and me go on my favourite roller coaster.

Leela Melodie Millar (8)
Holy Trinity CE Primary School, Cheltenham

I Am Myself And Nobody Can Change It

I am happy, I am curious, I love pizza,
I like football, I feel small inside,
I am lanky, I feel greedy when I am jealous,
I am playful, I am me, I am energetic like a puppy,
I love my little brother Theo,
I am sad when I am hurt,
I am me and no one can change anything about me.

Luca Castellini-Inniss (8)
Holy Trinity CE Primary School, Cheltenham

Untitled

I am me.
I'm the perfect actor.
I am me.
Magician - making rotten apples appear.
I am me.
I perfectly fractured an Airpod tracker.
I got into an accident today,
It was a burn on a slide.
I am me.

Zac Scott (8)
Holy Trinity CE Primary School, Cheltenham

I Am Me

I am grateful
I am caring for everyone
I am happy when I am loved
I give my dogs walks

I am friendly
I will always help people when they need it
I will never give up and be myself
I am loved.

Ruby Bruce (8)
Holy Trinity CE Primary School, Cheltenham

Me

O ssian is my name
S ongs, I really like songs
S uper happy, I may not look happy but I am
I am me
A t times I get very hungry
N ames of my friends are special to me.

Ossian Donnally (8)
Holy Trinity CE Primary School, Cheltenham

My Awesome Life

T he world of Tyrus...
Y ou are important to me!
R emembering friends' birthdays is my strength.
U nique sense of humour.
S mile that brightens up even the darkest of days.

Tyrus Chan (9)
Holy Trinity CE Primary School, Cheltenham

I Am Me

I am me,
I like my Xbox,
I like my family,
I like my friends,
I like my bedroom,
I like holidays,
I sometimes like a time to be quiet and calm.

Jesse Taylor (9)
Holy Trinity CE Primary School, Cheltenham

Happy

H appy all day
A mazing feeling
P erfect
P eople you talk to
Y es to the end.

Amelia Williams (8)
Holy Trinity CE Primary School, Cheltenham

Me

My life
I like Harry Potter
My favourite food is an apple
I have a very bad temper sometimes.

Martha Rufus (8)
Holy Trinity CE Primary School, Cheltenham

Me

A kennings poem

Violin player
Reading lover
Great mathser
Animal carer
Cat owner
Nature lover.

Effie Patterson-Brown (9)
Holy Trinity CE Primary School, Cheltenham

This Is Me

F ish are cute
L ove
Y appy
N ice
N ippy.

Flynn Workman (8)
Holy Trinity CE Primary School, Cheltenham

All About Painting!

P ainting is entertaining
A lways interesting or exciting
I t makes me feel happy
N ever dull or predictable
T aking time, but worth it!
E verything is paintable
R eally good fun!

Veronica Maguire (10)
Real Action Butterfly School, Queens Park

Swimming Is Part Of Me

Swimming smells like coral
Swimming tastes like extra salty cucumbers
Swimming feels like a warm hug
Swimming sounds silent underwater
Swimming pool is full of shiny water.

Faith Odunsi (7)
Real Action Butterfly School, Queens Park

Not Keen To Be Me

As soft as a feather and big a titan for my talents.
I am silent as for me I'm not keen to be as I am just meat and muscle.
So pure and insecure, just another grain at the beach or another planet orbiting the sun, we're all in it together coming and bowing.
I'm basically a raindrop in the sky,
I fall out of the cloud,
And I fall and fall as my life flashes before I hit the ground and die.
I'm not keen to be me just like the guy next to me.
Just a grain of rice, another grain of sand,
Just another piece of grass,
Just another leaf on a tree,
Not keen to be me.

Qotayba Alabbas (11)
Udston Primary School, Hamilton

This Is Me

My mum is the woman I admire the most
I'm a chatterbox, but am kind and funny
My eyes are as green as the grass
I'm as tall as a giraffe
When I grow up, I want to be a photographer
And my photos will be as clear as water
I dream of one day photographing the mouth-dropping landscapes
Of the culturally-rich country which is Portugal
And is also my country
When I first came to Scotland, I despised living here
But now I have been here for multiple years
I really enjoy living in Scotland.

Catarina Vitorino (11)
Udston Primary School, Hamilton

This Is Me

My favourite thing about me is
Playing with my friends
And going out with my friends
What makes me feel better
When I feel sad
Is my friend Aarya
She makes me feel better
When I am sad
And it makes me so happy
If I feel sick
She makes me feel
So much better
My dream for the future
Is to make
Everyone happy
And to be kind
To everyone
To stop bullying
And hurting some people
Because they don't know
Where to live

And they don't
Have any food to live
And stay warm
In the cold.

Jessica Payne (11)
Udston Primary School, Hamilton

Myself

I have big blue eyes and lovely blonde hair,
A small nose and a big heart.
My personality is as big as an elephant
But I am as small as a baby monkey.
I am fast like an eagle in the sky,
I sing to the trees as they sing to me.
I run and play all day with the birds,
I can share all my worries and doubts.
I play with the cheeky foxes,
Sometimes doing naughty stuff,
But I redeem myself by having fun
With the loving dogs
That love me so much.
They are like family.

Lacey Cairney Mullen (11)
Udston Primary School, Hamilton

This Is Me!

K ind, always there for others.
A ctive, very sporty and enjoys it.
C aring, I have a shoulder for you to cry on.
E nthusiastic, always positive and bright.
Y outhful, I have meaning

L oving, I love my friends and family.
E nergetic, always hyper and loves to annoy people.
I ndependent, I like getting my work done.
G rateful, I'm always happy with what I get.
H opeful, always has hopes and dreams.

Kacey-Leigh Henderson (11)
Udston Primary School, Hamilton

My Poem

A rtistic, angry when I'm woken up in the morning!
V ery, very, very chatty!
A mazing at drawing and loves cheerleading!
-
L aughs when my dogs prance about like ballerinas!
O ver the moon to make new friends!
U pset when I think about my old rabbit.
I ncredible and I will always be here to chat!
S weet like a strawberry, but sometimes sour,
A ctive and flexible, hard-working and creative.

Ava-Louise Mccarthy (11)
Udston Primary School, Hamilton

I Am Who I Am

I am adventurous
I am a bookworm
I am who I am and I like who I am
I love when I achieve something that I've dreamed about for years
It's like seeing your best friend after months of them not being there
I am who I am
I am mischievous
I am a Taylor Swift fan
I am who I am
And I like who I am
I am short, mighty and feisty
Like a tiger!
I am who I am
And I like who I am
And I always will!

Amy Williamson (10)
Udston Primary School, Hamilton

All About Me

I ntelligent and instrumental and will never give up
S ending kindness and respect to everyone in the world
A ppreciative to my mum because without her I wouldn't be here
B rave like a lion hunting for its dinner
E nergetic like a lion cub playing with its siblings
L oving like how my mum loves me
L ikeable like my sister Lily
E nthusiastic like my sister Megan.

Isabelle Keenan (10)
Udston Primary School, Hamilton

My Dream

My dream is for me to tend to the animals that give me glee,
My dream is to be the best farmer I can be,
My dream is to help the creatures in need,
My dream is to care for those who cared for me,
My dream is my goal, the thing I look for,
My dream is to ride across the meadow on my trusted steed, move so fast I'll be the wind,
My dream, my dream is what I need to be.

Ayva Buchanan (11)
Udston Primary School, Hamilton

This Is Me

My favourite thing about me is that I love PE and I love playing with some friends.
The ingredients that make me are that I am kind, brave, friendly, helpful, encouraging
My dream for the future is that I want to make everyone feel happy and I want to be a footballer.
I admire Jessica Payne because she's my best friend among everybody.
She's my only friend.

Kaima Ugo-Okafor (11)
Udston Primary School, Hamilton

Rugby Is Me

I step onto that field knowing I'm gonna give it my all
I see my pal and we know, no matter a win or loss,
We will have tried our very best!
I see my teammates and tell them, "Come on!"
I feel a touch of pride being the captain.
I smell the fresh air and mud.
I can touch the small grip bits on the rugby ball.
This is it, here we go!

Manus Whelan (11)
Udston Primary School, Hamilton

This Is Me!

I'm very funny. I like people. I have a lot of friends.
This is me.
I have a little brother and a little sister.
This is me.
I do things that I don't mean in a bad way.
This is me.
I fall out with people and have arguments with my friends.
This is me.
I have amazing best friends that I love, and I take care of them.
This is me!

Katie Jack (11)
Udston Primary School, Hamilton

About Me

A nimals are so cool like a rapper
L oving like a puppy
E nthusiasm is like a monkey
X -ray me to see what bones I'm made of
A mazing like a brilliant goal
N oisy like a parrot
D efender of my peers
E ach bit of my memory is very important
R eally intelligent like a calculator.

Alexander Shaw (10)
Udston Primary School, Hamilton

Luna Is Living Life

I admire my dog
Because she is as fluffy as a cloud
She is like a big ball of cotton candy
Her eyes are as blue as the sky
Her favourite things are to lick me
And annoy me when I try to sleep
But no no no more sleep for me
"Luna you horror!" I say
But at the end of the day
It's too hard to be annoyed.

Cooper Allan (10)
Udston Primary School, Hamilton

I Am Me!

My long luscious hair, my mum says is beautiful.
I'm like a cat, loving hugs from my gran.
I run with horses all day and all night.
I go up to bed and see the moon shine bright.
The next day will be a delight.
So let's become bright.
Like the glowing beams of moonlight and the armour of a knight.
Be yourself!

Hannah Marie Aitken (10)
Udston Primary School, Hamilton

All About Me!

L earning is like my life, you always learn from your mistakes and learn something new every day.
U nforgettable that kindness comes from your heart, not from your mouth.
C onfident as an actor walking on a red carpet.
Y ou can do anything if you put your intelligent mind to it.

Lucy Cochrane (10)
Udston Primary School, Hamilton

This Is Me

My family are the people I love the most,
I'm a funny man who is strong and fast,
I'm as fast as an F1 car racing around,
My brain is as small as a pebble,
My dream in the future is to be a terrific train driver,
The ingredients to make me are funny, silly and a little bit dumb.

Luka Mills (11)
Udston Primary School, Hamilton

All About Me

E nergetic, always hyper and upbeat
I nspirational, comes up with bright and colourful ideas
L oving, always care and love my family
I nclusive, likes to include people
D arling of my mother and father
H appy, always joyful and gets excited easily.

Eilidh Murdoch (11)
Udston Primary School, Hamilton

This Is Me!

L oving and helpful towards my parents
U nique and creative in school when I am doing art
C aring and sharing towards my friends and family
Y oung and intelligent like my big sister

B rave and sporty in boxing, trying out new workout methods.

Lucy Berney (11)
Udston Primary School, Hamilton

All About Faith

F aithful and into music, and really into arty stuff,
A nimal lover, annoyed easily, gets anxious when travelling,
I ndependent Irish,
T ikTok addicted, troublemaker trustworthy,
H appy most of the time, honest and hopeful.

Faith Tilly (11)
Udston Primary School, Hamilton

Me

My small round head that my mum says is cute.
My small and short body.
My long, speedy legs that make me run as fast as a horse and jump as high as the roof.
I get very grumpy in the morning.
Playing in goal in the MUGA and for my football team.

Nathan Gourlay (11)
Udston Primary School, Hamilton

Me, Myself And I

M ighty and helpful.
I ntelligent and caring.
R esilient and brave.
R esponsible with a kind heart.
E xtravagant with a love of sport.
N urturing and never gives up in the presence of a challenge.

Mirren Telfer (11)
Udston Primary School, Hamilton

People Think I'm Good At Football But I'm Not

I'm a funny chap, who is kind and true,
Some people think I'm good at football, but I think I'm not,
My friend Corey is way better than me,
He is the only one who passes to me,
Corey says I'm good but I'm not.

Harry Kennedy (10)
Udston Primary School, Hamilton

This Is Me

My mum is the one I admire the most
I am kind, smart, funny, creative and brave
That's what makes me, myself and I unique
My dream is to be an amazing police officer
And a great Lego maker too.

Hannah Rashid (10)
Udston Primary School, Hamilton

All About Junior

J olly, funny and enjoyable.
U nbeatable in a challenge.
N ice, chill and naughty.
I ntelligent, smart and adventurous.
O ptimistic.
R eally cool.

Junior Rushford (11)
Udston Primary School, Hamilton

This Is Me

A dventurous and helpful like a well-behaved dog.
D etermined, I never give up.
A lways will make you laugh and smile at all costs.
M enacing, always up to something.

Adam Paterson (11)
Udston Primary School, Hamilton

Sam

S uper when it comes to listening, sports and work.
A ctive even when it comes to the cold, damp days.
M indful when it comes to using my wild imagination to imagine pictures.

Sam McKeating (10)
Udston Primary School, Hamilton

Me!

C old like ice, really like rice.
O ne day, one PlayStation.
L ittle time for air, always in my room.
E xcited, hopping like a hare, never seen a loom.

Cole Higgins (11)
Udston Primary School, Hamilton

What Makes Me Me!

My big blue-green eyes
My personality
Makes me.

My intelligence
My creativity
Makes me.

My enthusiasm
My clothing style
Makes me.

Allanah McCourt (11)
Udston Primary School, Hamilton

All About Me

M y bright blue ocean eyes that sparkle like the night sky.
Y oung and intelligent, smart and funny.
A rty and creative, active and sporty.

Mya McDade (10)
Udston Primary School, Hamilton

Tedi

T he time when I play my PlayStation
E at food first, but
D id you know I like cheese?
I magine you put it in a sentence.

Tedi Alla (11)
Udston Primary School, Hamilton

All About Me

My eyes are as blue as the sky,
My hair is yellow like a lemon,
I have a nose like a button,
And my favourite colour is green like the grass.

Lexi Pollock (11)
Udston Primary School, Hamilton

Me

I am a speeding train,
Racing down the track,
My hair is as brown as a brownie,
My right foot is better than my left foot.

Rhys MacMillan (9)
Udston Primary School, Hamilton

All About Me

A ctive and arty
N urturing and nice
N oisy and naughty, but nice
A ggressive and agreeable.

Anna Gray (11)
Udston Primary School, Hamilton

The Speeding Train

I'm a speeding train
Going round on a train track
And going so fast
Like a racing car on a train track.

Corey Finlay (10)
Udston Primary School, Hamilton

This Is Me!

I'm a speeding train
Racing around a cornfield
Until I saw a shadow
And then it disappeared.

Charlie Goldie (10)
Udston Primary School, Hamilton

This Is Me!

In a world full of colours bright,
I am a girl who wants to shine with the light.
Kind and helpful, always there,
With a heart that's full of care.

I love horses, graceful and strong,
And dogs, loyal all day long.
I am like a rainbow,
Bringing joy to all who see my colours.

With a sense of humour, there's no doubt.
I am a wonderful friend who will help you shine
bright like the star you are.

This is me.

Nyrenah Mayne-Jenkins (8)
Woodburn Primary School, Carrickfergus

The Skate Park

When I go to the skatepark, sometimes I fall.
Then other times I stand tall.
When I am scared, I hold on to a friend.
But it is always okay in the end.
When I'm going down the ramp, I feel a bit damp.
When I got to the skatepark, I learn new tricks.
I love to show off.
I have a lot of fun in the sun.
At the skatepark.

Frankie Mckinney (8)
Woodburn Primary School, Carrickfergus

YoungWriters
Est. 1991

YOUNG WRITERS INFORMATION

We hope you have enjoyed reading this book – and that you will continue to in the coming years.

If you're the parent or family member of an enthusiastic poet or story writer, do visit our website **www.youngwriters.co.uk/subscribe** and sign up to receive news, competitions, writing challenges and tips, activities and much, much more! There's lots to keep budding writers motivated!

If you would like to order further copies of this book, or any of our other titles, then please give us a call or order via your online account.

Young Writers
Remus House
Coltsfoot Drive
Peterborough
PE2 9BF
(01733) 890066
info@youngwriters.co.uk

Join in the conversation!
Tips, news, giveaways and much more!

YoungWritersUK YoungWritersCW youngwriterscw

Scan me to watch the This Is Me video!